COACHING
YOUR
EMPLOYEES

COACHING YOUR EMPLOYEES

Nancy Stimson

KOGAN
PAGE

To Michael, Holly and Vicky

First published in 1994

Apart from any fair dealing for the purposes of research or private study, or criticism or review, as permitted under the Copyright, Designs and Patents Act, 1988, this publication may only be reproduced, stored or transmitted, in any form or by any means, with the prior permission in writing of the publishers, or in the case of reprographic reproduction in accordance with the terms of licences issued by the Copyright Licensing Agency. Enquiries concerning reproduction outside those terms should be sent to the publishers at the undermentioned address:

Kogan Page Limited
120 Pentonville Road
London N1 9JN

© Nancy Stimson 1994

British Library Cataloguing in Publication Data

A CIP record for this book is available from the British Library.

ISBN 0-7494-1182-1

Typeset by BookEns Ltd, Baldock, Herts.
Printed and bound in Great Britain by Clays Ltd, St Ives plc.

Contents

Acknowledgements   **9**

How to Use This Book   **11**

Blueprint – The Why, What, Who and How of Coaching

1. Why Coach Your Employees?   **13**
Summary *13*; Coaching – why bother? *13*;
Coaching is . . . *14*; Coaching is not . . . *16*;
Benefits of coaching for you *16*;
Benefits for your employees *17*;
Benefits for your company *18*

2. Why Doesn't it Happen?   **19**
Summary *19*; Cinderella *19*;
Barriers to being coached *20*;
Barriers to coaching *21*;
Overcoming the Barriers *21*; Suggested answers *23*

3. What Are Coaching Situations?   **24**
Summary *24*; Some conversations *24*;
Work-based *27*; Completing a task *27*;
Learning objective *27*; Planned *28*;
Strengths and weaknesses *29*;
Partnership relationship *29*;
Suggested answers *30*

4. **Who Needs Coaching?**   31
    Summary 31; Wage negotiation post-mortem 31;
    High priority needs 33; Suggested answers 34

5. **Who Should Coach?**   35
    Summary 35; The ideal coach 35;
    Subject or task expert 37; Qualifications 37;
    Position of authority 37; Self-confidence 38;
    Desire to learn 38; Friendly relationship 38

6. **How Do You Coach?**   39
    Summary 39; Coaching is a process 39;
    Process chart 40; Preparation 41;
    Briefing discussion and agreeing the contract 42;
    Completing and monitoring the task 43;
    Review discussion 44; Practice and follow-up 44

Foundation-Stone

7. **Your Attitude**   45
    Summary 45; Your experiences of being coached 45;
    You and your employees 46

Building Blocks – Coaching Skills

8. **Finding Time to Coach**   49
    Summary 49; The dilemma 49; How much time? 49;
    Priorities, priorities 50; Where does your time go? 51

9. **Identifying Learning Needs, Objectives and
    Approaches**   54
    Summary 54; Whose responsibility is it to identify
    learning needs? 54; What are learning needs? 55;
    What are learning objectives? 56;
    Knowledge/skills/attitudes 56;
    Suggested answers 59

10. **Identifying Coaching Opportunities**   60
Summary 60; Friday the 13th 61;
Sarah's opportunities for coaching 62;
Typical coaching opportunities 62;
Opportunities in your department 64

11. **Asking Questions**   66
Summary 66; Why ask questions? 66;
Types of question 69;
What if you don't get any answer? 69;
Changing attitudes 70; Suggested answers 75

12. **Listening**   76
Summary 76; What is listening? 76;
Importance of listening 77;
How well do we listen? 77;
How much do you know about listening? 77;
Barriers to listening 78; L I S T E N 79;
Suggested answers 81

13. **Observing**   83
Summary 83; Optical illusions 83;
How do we observe? 83; Observing work 85;
Charts 86; Answers 86

14. **Giving Feedback**   87
Summary 87;
Feedback, learning and motivation 88;
Suggestions for giving feedback 89;
Praise 90; Criticism 91; Some situations 92;
Suggested answers 93

15. **Explaining**   94
Summary 94; Bob's problem 94;
Employee perspective 96;
Suggestions for effective explanations 97;
Bob's problem avoided 97; Suggested answers 98

16. **Demonstrating**   100
     Summary *100*; Nellie *100*; Preparation *101*;
     Modelling the desired behaviour *102*;
     Trying the behaviour *103*; Feedback *103*

17. **Setting Goals and Standards**   104
     Summary *104*; Comparing goals and standards *104*;
     Manager/Employee agreement *105*;
     End-results *105*; Measurement *106*;
     Performance level *107*; Written documents *107*;
     Suggested answers *108*

18. **Gaining Commitment**   109
     Summary *109*; More than good intentions *109*;
     Management style *109*; Skills *111*;
     Your commitment *112*

Tools

19. **Checklists**   114
     Preparing to coach *114*; Briefing discussion *115*;
     Monitoring the task *116*; Review discussion *117*;
     Following up *118*

20. **Your Action Plan**   119

Further Reading from Kogan Page   121

Acknowledgements

I should like to thank Dennis Bessant, Ian Brown, Peter Cross, Peggy Edwards, Barry Watson and Georgina West for reading the various drafts of this book and for their very constructive feedback, and, in particular, Peggy Edwards for all her help and coaching over the years.

How to Use This Book

This book is a basic guide to coaching for managers. Read it in one sitting (it will probably take you about two to three hours), or dip into particular chapters according to your interests. Each chapter starts with a summary, so that you know what it covers.

Use the book to *build a staircase to success* for you and your people. The blueprint chapters (1–6) will help you think through your own views on coaching, as these form your foundation-stone (Chapter 7). Then add the building-block skills (Chapters 8–18), and use the tools (Chapters 19–20) to check your progress.

Treat the book as a store of tips and suggestions; you almost certainly won't want to use all of them, so adopt, and adapt, the ones you think will work for you and your people. Try your hand, too, at the many exercises, as it is interesting and illuminating to compare your views with someone else's. (By the way, my 'suggested answers' are just that – my views, based on what I have learnt and observed. I think they are right, but feel free to disagree if they don't match your experience – there are very few invariably 'right' answers in management.)

The case-studies all focus on the finance department of a small widget manufacturer. Sarah is finance manager, and her department comprises:

- An accountant, Paul, who is her official deputy
- Two accounts clerks, John and Martin
- An internal auditor, Carol
- A secretary, Ann.

Sarah has had a bad month. Friday the 13th was particularly fraught, starting with John's dismissal by Paul, and progressing through unsuccessful union wage negotiations to Paul's resignation, although this was later withdrawn. Sarah has also had to deal with the recruitment of Bob to replace John, a complaint about Carol, and the usual daily problems.

Throughout the book, we will eavesdrop on some of Sarah's conversations as she coaches her employees. Learn from her successes and mistakes by putting yourself in her place. Would you choose the same approach? Would it work with your people? If not, what *would* you do?

Finally, and most important of all, don't just read about it – do it. The more you practise coaching, the more you and your employees will benefit, and the more you will enjoy it!

CHAPTER 1

Why Coach Your Employees?

Summary

- Your success as a manager depends on the performance of your staff.
- Coaching is a conscious process of helping them to learn from their day-to-day job tasks.
- Coaching occupies the middle ground between teaching and everyday management feedback.
- Coaching is essential if people are to improve, or even maintain their performance.
- Coaching works! Its results can be identified.
- Coaching benefits you, your employees, and your company.

Coaching – why bother?

Have you ever:	Yes	No
• Had too much work and not enough time to do it in?	☐	☐
• Dreaded returning from holiday to an overflowing in-tray and a long tale of disasters?	☐	☐
• Had to explain away, or cover up, an employee's error?	☐	☐

- Been constantly interrupted by
  employees with minor queries? ☐ ☐
- Been passed over for promotion because
  there was nobody capable of taking over
  from you? ☐ ☐

If you answered 'Yes' to any of these questions, your employees need coaching. But coaching isn't just for when things go wrong. If an employee has successfully completed a project or come up with a solution to a problem, coaching will help him or her build on that success.

Even if (or rather, especially if) you are drowning in work which was required yesterday, coaching your staff may well be the best use of your time. *Your success as a manager depends wholly on the performance of your employees.* The better they perform, the easier your job and the greater your reputation.

Coaching is . . .

- Helping your people to learn from day-to-day job tasks, activities such as:
  - writing a report
  - representing their department at a meeting
  - handling queries
  - checking their own work
  - checking other people's work.
- A conscious, deliberate process which adds value to people's work experience, so that 'ten years' experience' can become much more than one year's learning repeated ten times.
- Essential, if your employees are even to *maintain* good performance, let alone improve it further. It would be wonderful if good performance was as predictable as turning on a tap – a guaranteed gush, after the initial training.

  Unfortunately, a gradually, or rapidly, reducing trickle is a more common result, as boredom and complacency clog up the pipes. Unfur them with continual coaching activities.

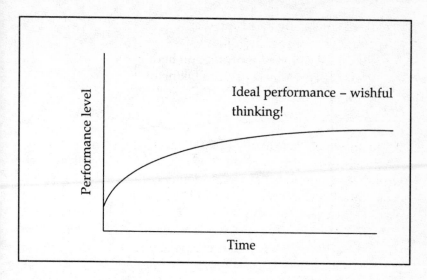

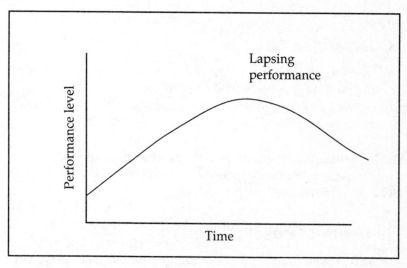

- Effective. It works! Its results can be identified, by you and (more importantly) by your employees. They are the things being done now which could not be done last month, or last year.

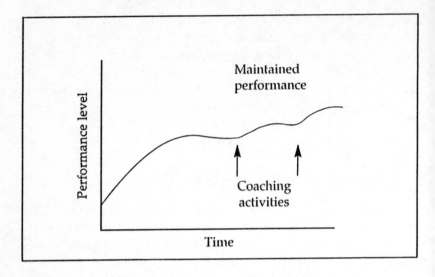

Coaching is not . . .

- Teaching or formal training, although many of the points in this book will apply equally to those activities.
- Ordinary everyday management feedback. Although informal, coaching is more deliberate and purposeful.

Coaching occupies the middle ground between these two techniques. Chapter 3 looks at the characteristics of typical coaching situations.

Benefits of coaching for you

Coaching is an investment, like buying a new computer system, a long-term strategy for success – your success, that of your employees, and that of your company. Some benefits of coaching for you are:

- A more successful and productive department
- Greater confidence when delegating tasks to your employees

- Development of your own management skills
- A growing reputation as a 'developer of people'
- Less time-consuming firefighting, allowing you to spend more time on your own development.

These in turn leading, possibly, to:

- Promotions and salary increases!

Benefits for your employees

But will your employees take kindly to the idea? Or will they resent what they see as your interference, and feel that you are just trying to squeeze extra work out of them? In other words, might coaching *demotivate* them?

Usually, no. The better people understand and can perform an activity, the more they enjoy it. Fundamentally, very few employees *want* to do a bad job – it's frustrating, a waste of time; and typically, has to be done all over again.

So any move to help an employee improve performance is normally welcome – and personal coaching can be the most welcome of all. You are making a positive affirmation that your employee is worth your time and trouble.

Benefits for employees include:

- The recognition of their importance to you, the department and the company
- The development of their skills
- Growing satisfaction as they improve their performance
- Greater interest in their tasks
- Greater independence and responsibility for their work
- A growing ability to take on more varied, interesting and challenging tasks.

Leading, possibly, to:

- Promotions and salary increases!

Benefits for your company

These include:

- Better motivated and developed employees
- Better motivated and developed managers.

Leading, not possibly but *definitely*, to:

- Better quality products and processes
- Greater profits.

CHAPTER 2
Why Doesn't it Happen?

Summary

- Coaching is, though it should not be, the Cinderella of the development business.
- Employees' and managers' fears about the coaching process may inhibit it from happening.
- This may lead to a spiral of deteriorating performance.
- Coaching, on the other hand, leads to a spiral of growth.

Cinderella

If coaching is such a good thing, why don't we do more of it?

Firstly because coaching may seem the poor relation of the development business – cheap and unglamorous when compared to abseiling down mountains, residential seminars in the capitals of Europe, or theoretical courses which will give you an impressive string of letters after your name.

Well, coaching is certainly cheap in direct costs, it is based on the workaday job, and it is nothing if not practical. But the results of coaching can be identified, can often be measured against established performance standards, and can even lead to nationally recognised vocational qualifications.

Barriers to being coached

The second reason is that, although I have so far stressed the benefits of coaching, there are also some very understandable fears and barriers for both the employee and the coach.

According to Paul's job description, he is supposed to supervise the two accounts clerks in the finance department. Paul has had no previous experience of supervision, and, despite having attended a training course for supervisors, he tends to avoid his responsibilities as supervisor and leave it all to Sarah. Paul genuinely wants to improve his supervisory performance and recognises that he needs coaching, but . . .

What feelings do you think might make Paul reluctant to be coached? List your views below, and turn to page 23 to compare them with mine.

-
-
-
-
-
-

Barriers to coaching

What about from Sarah's perspective? What fears might she have? My views are given on page 23.

-
-
-
-
-
-

Overcoming the barriers

As you can see, I think that both sets of barriers are very similar. And often all that is needed for coach and employee to overcome their fears is to acknowledge this similarity to themselves, or even better to each other. Deliberately reminding yourself of the benefits of coaching (and the dangers of not coaching) is also useful. Because, if you let the fears take over, there is a rapid descent down the slippery slide of lapsing performance to the bottomless pit below.

But coaching reverses the process, and builds that staircase to success for you and your people.

Try it for yourself. For in the end, the best encouragement to more coaching is a successful coaching experience.

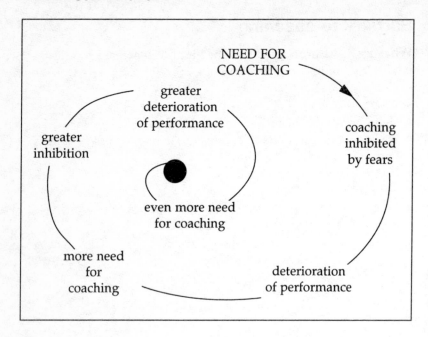

OR:

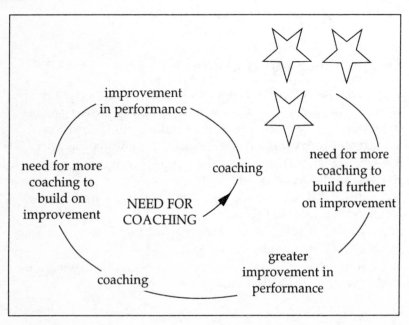

Suggested answers

Paul might fear:

- Exposing his lack of skill
- Being criticised
- Being made to feel small
- Feeling let down (and looking naïve), if Sarah is not genuinely committed to helping him
- Not being *able* to improve
- Diminishing salary/job prospects, if the coaching goes badly
- Not getting enough benefit (in terms of salary/job prospects), even if his performance does improve
- Spending time on coaching, and having to work harder (both to improve his performance and to make up for the coaching time).

Sarah might fear:

- Exposing her own lack of skill (especially if she believes she has to be expert in everything)
- The unpleasantness of criticising
- Playing God and sitting in judgement
- Feeling let down (and looking naïve), if Paul is not genuinely committed to learning
- Paul's performance not improving, despite her coaching
- Paul's performance improving, so that he becomes a rival for *her* job
- Not being able to meet Paul's salary/job prospect expectations
- Spending time on coaching, and having to work harder to make up for this time.

CHAPTER 3
What Are Coaching Situations?

Summary

Coaching situations typically:

- Are work-based
- Involve completing a task
- Have a definite learning objective
- Are planned in advance
- Use the employee's strengths and weaknesses to promote learning
- Reflect a partnership relationship between coach and employee, and a supportive management style.

Some conversations

Which of these conversations illustrate coaching discussions?

A

> Sarah: John, I want to talk to you about our payroll system. I've spoken to Paul and he suggested that I talk directly with you. The personnel manager has asked me to see if we can incorporate pensions administration into our payroll system. You know more than I do about the system, so I wondered if you would like to take on the project? What do you think?

> John: Yes, I'd like to do that, but I'm not sure how to set about it.
>
> Sarah: Well, let's talk about what the personnel manager wants from us, and see what ideas you have.

B

> Sarah: Hallo, Ann. How did the training course go?
>
> Ann: OK. I enjoyed it and found it interesting.
>
> Sarah: Good. Do you have a few minutes to talk me through what you found most helpful, and how you plan to use it on the job? Before you went on the course, you mentioned that you particularly hoped to get some ideas on how to prioritise your tasks. How are you planning to tackle that now?

C

> Carol (finishing dry run of presentation): And that is the main message that I want to leave you with, ladies and gentlemen. Thank you very much for your attention. Are there any questions?
>
> Sarah: Well done, Carol. That's strong and punchy, and should keep the audience's attention very well. However, there was just one point where I didn't quite follow your argument. When you were talking about . . .

D

> Paul (at coffee machine): Oh, Sarah, I'm glad I bumped into you. I wanted to ask you if you had received any reactions from the union about my wage settlement proposals.
>
> Sarah: Not yet, Paul, but I'm planning to incorporate them into the negotiation package. I've been meaning to say that I thought you did a really thorough job with those proposals. Where on earth did you find all that information about other companies' pay and productivity ratios?

E

> Martin (speaking on telephone): I'm sorry, Mr Jones, he's out of the office . . . I'll ask him to call you as soon as he gets in . . . No, I'm afraid I don't know when he'll be back . . . Goodbye, Mr Jones.
>
> Sarah: Who was that, Martin? What did he want?
>
> Martin: Mr Jones from Stewart and Jackson. He wanted to talk to Paul.
>
> Sarah: I see. Would it have been possible for anyone else to help him?
>
> Martin: I never thought to ask him that. He did sound a bit impatient. John is working with Paul on the Stewart and Jackson account. Perhaps I'd better ask him to call Mr Jones if Paul's not back soon.

All of these are coaching discussions. Coaching is helping an employee to learn and develop, by deliberately taking advantage of opportunities which arise in the day-to-day job.

Work-based

From a project to revise the payroll system to an impromptu lesson on answering the telephone, all jobs offer many learning opportunities, both large and small. The small daily opportunities may indeed, in the end, produce the most results. It's so much easier to climb the staircase to success when there are many shallow steps, rather than fewer steep ones!

Completing a task

Discrete tasks, however small, are more useful than ongoing situations. Coach and employee have a target to aim at; they can identify and reflect on the successful completion of the task, and build on this success with further discrete tasks. Look back on the coaching discussions at the beginning of the chapter, and pick out the tasks involved. (These are listed below.)

Learning objective

The purpose of coaching isn't just the completion of a particular task – its more fundamental aim is the longer term development of an employee's skills. In the examples at the beginning of the chapter, what do you think could be the intended learning objectives to be achieved through the coaching process? (Suggested answers are on pages 29–30.)

Task	Possible learning objectives
A Identifying how to revise the payroll system, making recommendations, getting them implemented	

B Attending training course	
C Delivering presentation	
D Completing proposals for wage settlement negotiations	
E Handling phone call from Mr Jones	

These possible objectives may not seem immediately obvious, but they, and many others, could all be achieved through the coaching situations.

Even if you haven't consciously formulated learning objectives when you coach an employee, they are probably hovering at the back of your mind. Bring them out into the open. The more you *and your employee* are aware of those learning objectives, the more easily can you achieve them.

Planned

Effective coaching benefits from pre-planning. Identify learning objectives; keep them in the forefront of your mind; and then deliberately seek out opportunities to achieve them.

Some opportunities do arise unexpectedly; for instance, the telephone call in conversation E. Even then, it was probably Sarah's awareness of Martin's deficiencies in answering the phone that triggered the questions, 'Who was that, Martin? What did he want?' The coffee machine chat (conversation D) is another example. If that hadn't occurred, Sarah would doubtless have created another opportunity.

Strengths and weaknesses

We tend, for obvious reasons, to concentrate efforts to improve performance on people's weak areas. Someone who cannot do the job needs to learn how. However, once a minimum adequate level has been reached, the biggest improvement in overall performance comes from concentrating on employees' strengths, enabling them to do even better what they already do well.

Look back on Sarah's comment to Paul at the coffee machine (conversation D). By explaining how he gathered the information about other companies' pay and productivity ratios, Paul will reinforce for himself a successful process, which means that he is more likely to use it again on other information-gathering assignments. Sarah will also be able to input ideas to make the process even more effective.

Partnership relationship

Coaching is not something one person *does* to another. Remember your schooldays: no teacher can *force* anybody to learn or improve. You and your employee have to work together as partners, with the employee as the senior partner! In many ways, to coach successfully you have to turn the normal organisation chart upside down. The manager-as-coach doesn't control the employee's efforts, but is in a supportive role, underpinning those efforts.

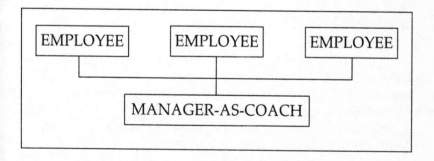

Suggested answers

Some possible learning objectives of the coaching situations are:

A
- Developing investigative skills, eg asking questions, sifting information
- Developing decision-making skills
- Developing presentation skills, eg report writing, oral presentations

B
- Applying training course information to Ann's job
- Reinforcing what she learnt on the course through discussion

C
- Structuring presentations logically
- Understanding audience's perspective
- Developing delivery skills

D
- Developing investigation, decision-making and presentation skills
- Reinforcing investigation skills by identifying what Paul has done well (specific objective of coffee machine chat)

E
- Successful handling of future phone calls
- Understanding caller's perspective.

CHAPTER 4
Who Needs Coaching?

Summary

- Everyone needs coaching.
- High priority needs include situations where:
  - performance improvement could bring a major benefit
  - failure to improve could lead to major problems
  - someone starts a new job, task or project
  - there are changes in equipment, processes or procedures.

Wage negotiation post-mortem

Managing director:	Well, we certainly lost that one! If I hadn't walked out when I did, we would have been real laughing stocks. Why on earth didn't you have all the information about the pension fund investments, Sarah?
Sarah:	Well, it's pretty complicated . . . Anyway, I didn't think we were going to discuss them. I thought personnel were supposed to have a 'special relationship' with the union, and that they understood our position.

Personnel manager:	I think they did understand our position, but did we understand theirs?
Sarah:	That's irrelevant. With the government constraints on us, we simply *can't* offer them any more money.
Managing director:	*More* money! For those lazy . . . *I* think we ought to cut our offer by half – that would teach them.
Personnel manager:	You can't do that! It's just insulting. We need to see if there is any common ground between us.
Managing director:	Common ground! Whose side are *you* on? Ours or theirs?

Who could benefit from coaching in this situation? What knowledge, skills or attitudes need improving? Some answers are suggested on page 34.

	Needs coaching? Y/N	**Knowledge, skills or attitudes needing improvement**
Managing director		
Sarah		

Personnel manager		

Senior as well as junior staff, managers as well as subordinates, may benefit from coaching. This is just as true in less dramatic situations than a failed negotiation. If that negotiation meeting had been successful, the managing director, Sarah and the personnel manager would still have been able to improve their performances as negotiators, by coaching each other in a post-mortem review of the meeting. Team coaching is a great method of team-building too.

High priority needs

As we saw in the first chapter, we all need to learn throughout our working lives, to avoid the dangers of stagnation and to keep our work performance from deteriorating. Beyond this, however, some situations are particularly critical:

- Where improvement could bring major benefits, such as a new contract
- Where failure to improve could lead to major problems, for example in this negotiation situation
- When somebody starts a new job, or takes on a new task or project
- When there are changes in equipment, processes or procedures.

Do any of your people fall into these high priority categories? If so, keep them particularly in mind while reading this book.

Suggested answers

All members of the negotiation team could benefit from coaching.

The managing director shows various counter-productive attitudes, such as:

- Seeing the negotiation as a battle, with winning (and making others lose) the desired outcome, rather than reaching mutually beneficial agreements
- Contempt for the workers
- Lack of trust in the personnel manager.

Sarah needs:

- Greater knowledge of the pension fund investments
- To improve her skills in preparing for negotiations
- To improve the inflexible attitude of seeing only her own position and objectives.

The personnel manager needs to build the trust of Sarah and the managing director – an essential skill.

CHAPTER 5
Who Should Coach?

Summary

- The ideal coach needs:
  - communication and information-gathering skills
  - a methodical approach
  - a degree of self-confidence
  - a personal desire to learn and help others develop
  - a relationship of mutual trust and respect with the employee.
- Depending on the situation, it may be useful or counter-productive to be:
  - a subject expert
  - in a position of authority.
- If employees are working towards external qualifications, coaches may themselves need some formal qualifications.

The ideal coach

With your own employees and situation in mind, how important would you consider the following qualities of a coach? (1 = not very important, 4 = essential.) Add to the list any other qualities you feel should be included, and rate those too.

	1	2	3	4
1. Subject or task expert				
2. Formal qualifications in training or coaching				
3. Communication skills				
4. Information-gathering skills				
5. Position of authority				
6. Self-confidence				
7. Methodical approach				
8. Desire to help others develop				
9. Desire to learn				
10. Friendly relationship between coach and employee				
•				
•				
•				
•				
•				

Any of these qualities *may* be important according to the situation. Some of them are self-evidently valuable; others, however, are worth discussing further.

Subject or task expert

This, perhaps surprisingly, is *not* necessarily an essential quality for a good coach. Consider the sporting environment. At top-level the person being coached is usually more expert than the coach. The same can be true in business: a generalist may be an excellent coach for a technical whiz-kid, and a mentor in a totally different department can open up new perspectives.

Too much expertise can, in any case, get in the way of success-ful coaching. It can be difficult for an expert to understand a novice's lack of understanding. However, a certain amount of subject knowledge is usually necessary, and the subject-expert coach does have a stock of experience and expertise to pass on.

Qualifications

Qualifications are a measure of achievement, but you don't need formal training qualifications to coach your staff. Coach-ing your employees isn't a job for the 'experts' in the training department, although they can be extremely helpful people for *you* to consult.

There is, however, one situation where a coach's external qualifications may be important. The development of NVQs and SVQs (National Vocational Qualifications and Scottish Vocational Qualifications) means that many people can use their work experience to help them gain nationally recognised qualifications. If any of your employees are working towards NVQs or SVQs, their progress has to be evaluated by extern-ally accredited 'assessors'. It can be very useful if their coaches know what is involved, possibly even being accredited assessors themselves. Similarly, employees working on projects for busi-ness or management qualifications may need to be assigned to coaches or mentors with external qualifications.

Position of authority

Your authority may be useful in obtaining, for your employee, the resources and authority necessary to complete the task.

Also, you, as the employee's manager, are normally the person best placed to identify or create coaching opportunities.

On the other hand, a non-authoritarian coaching relationship, where the coach and employee are *partners*, may be easier to establish between peers, or with technical experts or mentors in other functions. In the negotiation post-mortem in the previous chapter, each member of the negotiation team could informally act as coach to the others. This is often a feature of team debriefings.

Your role as manager does of course change depending on whether you, or somebody else, coaches your staff. The manager who is also coach needs to put aside the consciousness of authority, and to view the process as the creation of a learning *team*. The manager whose employees are coached by other people needs to welcome those others into the learning team.

Self-confidence

Essential! It is extremely difficult to imbue others with confidence if you do not believe in yourself. Over-confidence, however, is another matter.

Desire to learn

The best coaches are enthusiastic coach-ees. Always keen to learn, they constantly seek out opportunities for *being* coached. Indeed, coaching an employee is, in itself, often a two-way development process, with the coach learning as much as the employee (for instance, by improving coaching and communication skills, and by gaining a different perspective).

Friendly relationship

While this is useful, it is by no means essential. You don't need to go down to the pub with your employee, or debate the merits of your favourite football teams. However, coach and employee *do* need to have, or build, a relationship of mutual trust and respect.

CHAPTER 6
How Do You Coach?

Summary

Coaching is a cycle. The process involves:

1. Preparation – identifying learning needs and objectives
   - identifying coaching opportunities
   - obtaining necessary resources and authority
2. Briefing discussion and agreeing the contract
3. Completing and monitoring the task
4. Review discussion
5. Practising what has been learnt, following-up, then identifying any further learning needs, and so back to step 1.

Coaching is a process

In a sense, the whole of this book is about how you coach, so why a separate chapter with the same heading?

One of coaching's plus points is that it is an informal activity. Often, you may just have a quick chat with an employee, catching a minor problem before it escalates, or reinforcing good practices so that the employee remembers and repeats them.

But those quick chats don't happen in isolation. There *is* a process involved. You may at first find it difficult to identify the different steps of the process in your impromptu coaching discussions, because they are not always conscious in your mind. And indeed, the briefing, monitoring and review steps may

Process chart

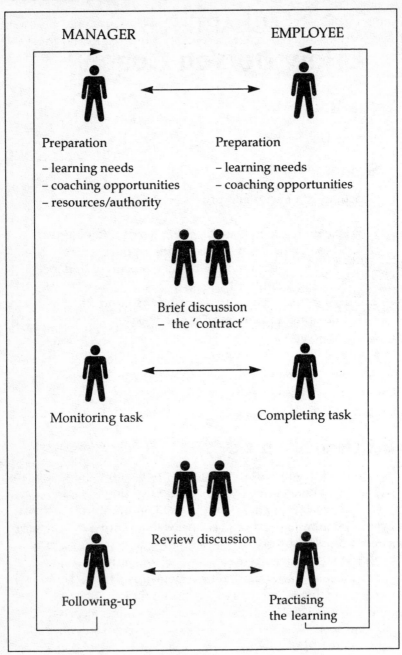

MANAGER

EMPLOYEE

Preparation

- learning needs
- coaching opportunities
- resources/authority

Preparation

- learning needs
- coaching opportunities

Brief discussion
– the 'contract'

Monitoring task

Completing task

Review discussion

Following-up

Practising
the learning

sometimes merge into just one or two discussions. But be aware of the different stages, especially preparation and follow-up – this will help you and your employee make the most impromptu of chats really productive.

Preparation

This stage consists of:

- Identifying learning needs and objectives
- Identifying coaching opportunities
- Obtaining necessary resources and authority.

This is largely common sense. Learning needs and objectives do not have to be 'big items', and identifying coaching opportunities is a matter of developing the frame of mind where they become obvious to you. Because these are essential coaching skills, further tips are given in Chapters 9 and 10.

Once you have identified the opportunity, clear any obstacles from the employee's path by obtaining the necessary resources and authority in advance. The employee will have more confidence and commitment if you make these arrangements in front of him or her. It only takes a few simple phone calls.

Sarah:	Alex, I'm asking John to look into how we can incorporate pension administration into our payroll system. Could you or one of your people spend a bit of time with him, please, outlining your needs? He has my authority to agree immediately to any procedural changes which don't involve reprogramming the system. He will be making recommendations about anything which requires system changes.

Briefing discussion and agreeing the contract

Coaching discussions, however informal, should never be treated casually. They are learning events. How well do *you* learn when you are:

- Hungry?
- Sitting on an uncomfortable chair?
- Too hot or cold?
- Tired?
- Overworked?
- Worried about something?

Ideal coaching sessions, both briefing and review, are:

- Short
- In a comfortable physical environment
- Timed for the employee's convenience.

As with any interview, ensure that there are no outside distractions, and arrange your furniture so that it doesn't inhibit free discussion. Many people find desks a barrier to communication. However, if you feel awkward seated anywhere else, don't feel obliged to conform to the low-coffee-table-and-armchairs convention. Instead, try positioning your desk so that you and the employee can sit diagonally across a corner.

The purpose of the briefing discussion is for the employee to understand clearly what needs to be done and why it needs doing, in terms of both task and learning objectives.

The briefing discussion establishes the 'contract' between you and the employee. You agree what the employee will be doing. You also agree, even if you never mention this directly, your own role, as supporter or dictator.

Coaching should help your employees to *grow*. The more you dictate and take over, the more you stunt that growth. What happens if you lecture the employee, who then learns the lesson by rote? Here is Paul trying to coach Ann in how to use medians in a monthly report which she prepares on his behalf.

> Paul: To complete this column, Ann, look at all the totals on this page and on the previous page. You count how many totals have been calculated and put them in ascending order. Then you . . .

Ann may follow Paul's instructions in this instance, but, because she hasn't understood what is really involved, may be unable to apply them in any other context. Instead of dictating:

- Try to identify what the employee understands already and build on that understanding.
- Aim to give sufficient guidance without being prescriptive.
- See that the employee has all necessary background information, and has thought through any problems that may arise.
- Get the employee to do about half the talking.

> Paul: So what do you think the purpose of this column is, Ann? . . . What information do you have to consider? . . . What do you need to do with it? . . .

Chapters 11–18 look at the skills involved in more detail.

Completing and monitoring the task

These are parallel activities with some interaction between the manager and the employee. How much interaction will vary considerably, but *judge this from the employee's standpoint, not yours*. Clearly, nobody likes to be left floundering; but it is frustrating, exasperating and generally infuriating to have your boss forever peering over your shoulder!

Most managers monitor work too closely. The more you found yourself dictating in the briefing discussion, the more you and your employee may assume that you will, and should, supervise closely, and the harder you may find to let go.

But let go you must. Let your monitoring be an elastic band around the task – you have ultimate control, but your employees can stretch the elastic to do things *their* way. Yes, you are responsible for the outcome, and yes, it does feel unnatural to sit back and allow mistakes to happen. However, mistakes in moderation are an important aspect of learning.

Review discussion

The aims of this are to establish:

- How well the task objectives were achieved – and what else needs doing
- How well the learning objectives were achieved – and what else needs doing
- How well you supported the employee in achieving these objectives – and what else you could do next time.

It should be the *employee* who establishes these points, who ideally will do about three-quarters of the talking, and who will set goals and plan future actions.

Practice and follow-up

Having developed a skill, the employee needs to use it or it will fade away. One of the purposes of the review discussion is to set goals for practising what has been learnt. However, as every music teacher knows, practice all too often just doesn't happen. Follow up, *regularly and frequently*. These follow-up chats may be very short (a few minutes may be plenty), but they do make a difference. Both of you, schedule them in your diaries to ensure that they aren't forgotten.

As a result of the follow-up, further learning needs may be identified, and so the cycle continues.

CHAPTER 7
Your Attitude

Summary

- Your feelings about coaching will often be influenced by your experiences of being coached.
- An attitude of genuine respect and regard towards your employees is the foundation-stone of your coaching relationship.

Your experiences of being coached

Try your hand at the following questions.

How did you learn to be a manager?

_____

_____

_____

Did anyone coach you? If so, how helpful did you find it?

_____

_____

_____

What are you able to do in your job now that you could not do, or could not do so well, last year?

_____

_____

_____

How did you learn or improve this activity?

_____

_____

_____

Did anyone coach you? If so, how helpful did you find it?

_____

_____

_____

Many managers feel that they have learnt their craft mainly on the job, by thinking about tasks and activities beforehand, carrying them out, and reflecting afterwards on how successful they were and why. Most managers also feel that they learn much better if they are able to talk the activity through and make use of someone else's experience, in other words if they are coached. If that is true for you, why not for your employees too?

But don't give up the idea if you haven't experienced coaching, or if you personally found it less successful. Your _employees_ will still benefit from coaching, from you or other people. It is your attitude to your employees which is critical. That is the foundation-stone of your coaching relationship.

You and your employees

To what extent do you agree with the following statements?

	Fully agree	Partly agree	In the middle	Partly disagree	Fully disagree
My employees:					
• Are intelligent					
• Want to learn					
• Want to work					
• Are capable of performing their jobs really well					
• Have jobs which provide scope for development					
• Trust and respect me.					
I:					
• Want to do my job better					
• Want to help my employees develop					
• Like to talk with my employees					
• Believe that the five most important things to say to employees are: 'Please', 'Thank you', 'Well done', 'I'm sorry' and 'I was wrong'					
• Trust and respect my employees					
• Can accept mistakes (within reason!) without losing my trust or respect for the employee.					

Count 5 points for every 'fully agree', 4 points for every 'partly agree', 3 points for every 'in the middle', 2 points for every 'partly disagree' and 1 point for every 'fully disagree'.

Have you scored 45 or more points? Then the foundation of your coaching relationship with your employees is securely laid.

Under 45 points? You need to consider how truly committed you are, to coaching and to your employees. Unless you genuinely respect and value your employees and yourself, the coaching process will be a sham, a matter of going through the motions. It will also be a failure, because employees will be quick to detect your lack of genuine commitment, and will themselves therefore not be committed. Reread the first part of this book and consider, *can you afford not to be committed to coaching?*

CHAPTER 8
Finding Time to Coach

Summary

- Coaching is an investment of time. In the long term, it will save time by reducing the need for firefighting.
- In the short term, it takes some time.
- To find time for coaching:
  - prioritise your activities
  - compare your ideal and actual use of time
  - treat coaching as a high priority.

The dilemma

I suggested in the first chapter that, the busier you are, the more important it is to invest time in coaching your staff. Development will increase their competence, their independence and their motivation, which means that you will need to spend less time firefighting and sorting out problems – in the long term.

However, in the short term, coaching itself takes time. So where can you find that time?

How much time?

It may be less than you fear. Consider how much of your day-to-day work is already spent helping your people, for instance when you:

- Delegate a task
- Demonstrate a task to an employee
- Check progress on a task
- Resolve work problems with employees.

These situations rarely take up long periods of time, but frequent short bursts of activity. The same is true of planned coaching.

Priorities, priorities

To find time to coach, check your priorities. List below six key areas of your job. 'Firefighting' and 'coaching staff' have been added to the end of the list for you.

Major activities	Ideal percentage of time
•	
•	
•	
•	
•	
•	
• Firefighting	
• Coaching staff	

Then estimate what percentage of your time you would ideally spend on each of these activities. And, although you are composing an ideal picture, tinge it with reality. Can you ever reduce firefighting to 0 per cent? Should all your percentages really add up to 100 per cent, or are there always some activities which don't fall into your key areas (not to mention lost time!)?

Where does your time go?

You may think you know, you may even be confident that the reality mirrors your ideal. But there is nothing like the acid test of a time-log.

This one (see pages 52–3) is divided into columns for your key areas plus firefighting and coaching. Check off each half or quarter of an hour under the appropriate column. If your activity doesn't fit into any of the eight columns, leave that time-slot blank. Next, at the end of the day/week/month, add up the time for each column, divide it by the number of hours worked (excluding lunch time), and multiply by 100. Then compare this with your ideal picture. Repeat this exercise regularly, as your priorities will change.

What if the reality is farther from the ideal than you would like? To gain more coaching time:

- Keep your ideal time picture in mind.
- Treat coaching as a priority activity.
- Schedule in coaching time at the start of each day (use your diary or a 'to do' list), before the fires start blazing.
- Use the fires themselves as coaching opportunities (see Chapter 10).

Coaching your Employees

	Monday Key areas 1 2 3 4 5 6 F C	Tuesday Key areas 1 2 3 4 5 6 F C	Wednesday Key areas 1 2 3 4 5 6 F C	Thursday Key areas 1 2 3 4 5 6 F C	Friday Key areas 1 2 3 4 5 6 F C
8.00					
9.00					
10.00					
11.00					
12.00					
13.00					

14.00	15.00	16.00	17.00	18.00

CHAPTER 9

Identifying Learning Needs, Objectives and Approaches

Summary

- *You* are responsible for identifying learning needs, but the more involved the employee the more committed he or she will be to the coaching.
- A learning need is the gap between desired and current performance.
- Learning objectives specify what knowledge, skills or attitudes should be developed to bridge the gap.
- The three basic types of learning (knowledge, skills and attitudes) require different coaching approaches.

Whose responsibility is it to identify learning needs?

The short answer is yours. Training departments can help you to carry out that responsibility but they don't take it away from you. However, do involve your employees in identifying learning needs (and coaching opportunities).

Compare these three situations:

A

> Paul: Ann, I know you always have difficulty with the median calculations in monthly reports, so I thought it would be useful to spend a little time together going through what's needed.

B

> Ann: Paul, is this right? I'm never quite sure about the median calculations for the monthly reports.
>
> Paul: Would you like to spend a little time going through it?

C

> Ann: Paul, is this right? I'm never quite sure about the median calculations for the monthly reports. Could you spend a little time going through it with me, please?

The more Ann identifies her own learning needs and initiates the coaching, the more committed to it she is likely to be.

What are learning needs?

A learning need is the gap between the performance you desire and the performance which is currently being achieved. Some people find this concept threatening and think it must imply that the current performance is bad, but you can equally have a gap between a current good performance and a desired outstanding one.

You may be familiar with the term 'training needs'. Learning needs are the same thing, but using the word 'learning' emphasises that:

- Training is not enough – we all know people who have been fully trained without learning a thing!
- As coach, you are a supporting partner – the starring role goes to the learner.

What are learning objectives?

I mentioned in Chapter 3 that a coaching assignment should have learning as well as task objectives. Learning objectives specify what should be done to meet the learning need.

Learning objectives should be expressed simply and specifically – the more specific the better, but take care not to get tangled up in *unnecessarily complex* measurements of performance. Measurements are an excellent way of clarifying statements (see Chapter 17) but they have their own dangers.

'Ann should write shorter minutes of meetings' may be quite sufficient, given that Ann and Sarah both understand how much shorter. 'Ann's meeting minutes should not exceed two pages' may be better, as long as everyone realises that a three-pager will be fine if the discussion warrants it. 'Ann's meeting minutes should be 20 per cent shorter' is likely to be counter-productive; it will take time to measure, and the emphasis on this precise measurement on its own implies that other aspects, such as the quality of the minutes, are not important.

Sometimes the learning need may, itself, constitute the objective, for instance, 'Ann needs to learn how to calculate medians.' But many learning needs are more complex.

Knowledge/skills/attitudes

There are three basic types of learning:

- Knowledge
- Skills
- Attitude.

Suggest what knowledge, skills or attitudes may require development to meet the following learning needs. My answers are given on page 59.

Learning need	Learning objectives		
	Knowledge	Skills	Attitudes
Paul needs to make appropriate supervisory decisions, within his sphere of authority			
Martin needs to be more helpful when answering phone calls			
Carol, as internal auditor, needs to win the confidence of departmental managers.			

The three basic types of learning (knowledge, skills and attitudes) are gained in different ways, and therefore require different types of coaching.

Learning knowledge

Useful sources of knowledge are:

- Explanations by coach or other employees (see Chapter 15)
- Written material, eg procedures, notices, books, periodicals
- Computer-based material, either written materials held on a computer, or special computer-based training materials
- Audio/video material. There is a wide range of commercial training materials, or you can create your own. This is particularly useful for needs which are shared by many people at different times, especially if they are scattered over different locations.

Learning skills

The best way of developing skills is through the demonstration process (see Chapter 16). Demonstration consists of:

- Preparing yourself and the employee
- Modelling the skill, with the employee observing you
- Getting the employee to try
- Giving feedback.

Repeat the last two or last three steps as often as necessary.

Learning attitudes

Getting people to change their attitudes is difficult and time-consuming. Nor is it always necessary. Successful changes in behaviour *can* occur without any change in underlying attitudes. But if a different attitude *is* needed, be content with gradual progress – rapid changes may not be genuine.

Productive changes in attitude usually come through careful questioning and listening (see Chapters 11 and 12) on the part of the coach. Telling someone to 'change your attitude' may indeed produce a change, but usually for the worse!

Suggested answers

Paul needs to:

- Know the limits of his authority and company staff procedures (knowledge)
- Make appropriate decisions and communicate them effectively (skills)
- Overcome his dependency on Sarah (attitude).

Martin needs to:

- Know the company 'house rules' for answering the phone (knowledge)
- Develop a pleasant voice and helpful manner (skills)
- Put himself in the customer's position (attitude).

Carol needs to:

- Question, listen and influence (skills)
- See the problems from the department managers' points of view (attitude).

CHAPTER 10
Identifying Coaching Opportunities

Summary

Typical coaching opportunities are:

- Something going wrong
- Successes
- Planned delegation
- Deputising for the manager
- Assisting the manager
- New jobs or promotions
- Temporary assignments and job rotation
- Special projects
- Relief cover
- Introduction of new systems
- After training activities and planned reading
- Developing other people
- Day-to-day job activities, such as: presentations, meetings and negotiations, reports, external contacts, any task which is currently supervised.

Friday the 13th

On Friday the 13th, Sarah got to the office early, hoping to spend the whole day preparing for the wage negotiation meeting with the union at 3.00 pm. However, her diary showed that she had a visit from a supplier of pensions administration software scheduled for 11.00 am, and a departmental meeting at 11.30 am (this was a weekly meeting which would normally last about half an hour – she unfortunately had had to cancel last week's meeting). She reckoned she could nevertheless just about complete her preparation in time for the afternoon meeting.

Sarah had, the day before, asked Paul to provide her with information about the pension fund investments in case the union representatives had any questions. The phone rang. It was Paul, but he hadn't got the information.

During the past few days, Paul had been trying hard to act more independently as a supervisor, but things hadn't gone well. When he had asked John, the day before, to get the investment details, John was very rude and told Paul that he was too busy working on the pension administration project for Sarah. Paul and John both got very heated. That morning, John had phoned in and insolently said he didn't feel like coming in to work that day. Paul got angry and told him not to bother to come back at all. Paul had informed personnel and was now telling Sarah. Sarah, forgetting the software supplier, arranged to see Paul before the departmental meeting.

As Sarah put the phone down, the personnel manager walked in and insisted on discussing Paul's action in dismissing John, which he felt could lead to an 'unfair dismissal' claim. The discussion was less than productive (partly because Sarah had half her mind on the pension fund investments) and went on until 11.00 am, when Ann announced that the software supplier had arrived. He proved impossible to get rid of, and Sarah arrived late at the departmental meeting. Paul, who had been waiting to see Sarah before the meeting, was also late . . . and angry. Sarah told Paul that she would not be able to see him until the next day. The departmental meeting dragged on, and it was early afternoon before Sarah, skipping lunch, started work on her preparation for the wage negotiation meeting, still without the investment information.

The afternoon meeting was a disaster, exposing Sarah's lack of knowledge about the pension fund investments. She got back to her office to find a letter of resignation from Paul, who claimed that she hadn't offered him the support he needed to do his job as supervisor.

Sarah's opportunities for coaching

Sarah clearly has problems as a manager! The point is that those problems all offer coaching opportunities. Which ones can you find in Sarah's disastrous day? My answers are given below.

-
-
-
-

Typical coaching opportunities

Sarah's opportunities fall under these typical categories:

- Something going wrong. Mistakes and failures can always be turned into learning opportunities. By helping Paul to understand the situation with John and to avoid similar problems in the future, Sarah could have restored his confidence in his supervisory skills and in her management.

- Planned delegation. Paul (and, if the dispute hadn't happened, John) could have met the software supplier. This would have had the advantage of involving Paul more closely in John's project.
- Deputising for the manager, as at the departmental meeting.
- Assisting the manager. Sarah badly needed to talk through her preparation for the union meeting before the event, so as to be able to field any awkward questions. Discussing her material with Paul would have helped her, as well as developing his knowledge and skills.

Other typical coaching opportunities may be:

- Successes. Analysing what went right and why, in order to repeat or even increase the success, boosts the employee's confidence and motivation, and develops the employee's expertise so that he or she can pass it on to others.
- New jobs or promotions.
- Temporary assignments and job rotation. These can be within your own department, between departments and even between companies.
- Special projects and working parties to examine particular issues.
- Introduction of new systems and equipment.
- Cover for sickness, holidays, etc.
- After any training activities, consolidating the learning and getting the employee to share it with others.
- Giving presentations.
- Planned reading programmes.
- Attending meetings and negotiations.
- Writing reports and proposals.
- Dealing with other departments or external contacts.
- Developing other people.
- Reducing or omitting supervision on any (currently supervised) task.

There are *lots* of potential coaching opportunities!

Opportunities in your department

This probably sounds fine in theory, but, you may be thinking, it's different for me because . . . It's not! *Every* function, *every* job lends itself to coaching. Here are some tips to help you recognise coaching situations.

- Have your employees keep work diaries, listing briefly what they have done and the outcomes. Review the diaries weekly with your employees. You will be amazed at the coaching possibilities.
- Do for your own job what you did for Sarah's. Think back to yesterday or one day last week, and list three coaching opportunities which you took advantage of.

Coaching opportunity	Employee concerned
•	
•	
•	

How about the ones that you could have used, but missed?

Coaching opportunity	Employee who could have benefited
•	
•	
•	

Missed opportunities matter. Each coaching opportunity that you seize is a step up that staircase to success – and each one that you miss is a step down.

• Finally, get in a bit of practice. Every day, pick half a dozen situations (three that you expect to happen or have planned in advance, and three as they occur), and ask yourself, as we did in Chapter 4, who would benefit from being coached in these situations. Soon every job will seem full of coaching opportunities.

CHAPTER 11
Asking Questions

Summary

- Different types of question will produce different sorts of answer.
- The principal types of question are:
  - open questions
  - closed questions
  - probes
  - reflective questions
  - leading questions
  - multiple questions.
- Don't rush in to fill the silence after a question.
- Questions are not only a means of getting information, they are also a powerful way of changing attitudes.

Why ask questions?

Obviously, to get answers, and, only slightly less obviously, different types of question will get different sorts of answer. Some types of question are more useful than others in coaching situations.

To illustrate these statements, let's see how Sarah coaches Paul (who withdrew his resignation) in how to use questions effectively when recruiting John's replacement.

Open questions
'Paul, what sort of questions would you ask a nervous candidate, to get him or her talking?'

This is an open question, inviting a free, reasonably lengthy and detailed response. Open questions, typically introduced by 'What', 'How' and 'Why', are the primary information-getting tools. They encourage people to think, and allow them to express their answers without restraint.

One point to consider, however – questions starting with 'Why' need special care. 'Paul, why do you want to ask that?' may put Paul on the defensive, which will hinder the information-getting process. An alternative phrasing (for example, 'Paul, what did you learn from that question?') may get round the problem.

Sometimes the answers to open questions are too long and rambling, and you then need to control these with specific closed questions and probes (see below).

Nevertheless, open questions are probably the most useful type of question for coaching. Unfortunately, they are used much less often than they should be, even by people who think they *are* using them. Time after time, in training-course role-plays, participants intend to use open questions, but instead express themselves almost entirely with statements and closed questions!

Closed questions
'Paul, do you need somebody with A levels?'

Closed questions invite short, specific answers, often 'Yes' or 'No' followed by an awkward silence. Paul *may* expand the answer, ('Yes, because . . .'), but Sarah will probably have to follow up with an open question ('What would be the advantages for us of A-level qualifications?'). Paul's response to this question will be less free than to an original open question, because the answer to the closed question has already pointed a particular direction (that A levels are necessary).

A closed question, however, can be very useful to:

- Curb a rambler
- Pin down a precise commitment ('Would you consider a school-leaver with A levels but no previous work experience?')

- Extract a specific piece of information ('Which A levels would be most useful to us?').

Probes
Probes are open or closed questions which get the employee to consider the issues more deeply. Don't be afraid to probe – it is a helpful, not an aggressive, technique.

'What about candidates without A levels but with relevant work experience?'

Reflective questions
'You consider that A levels are a good indicator of someone's ability to handle complex information – is that right?'

These questions reflect back the employee's view. They:

- Demonstrate that the coach understands the employee's position
- Summarise and clarify the main points
- Get the employee to explore the issue further.

Reflective questions can mirror both what is said and the underlying emotions ('Am I right in thinking that you also want us to be seen to be well qualified?'). But a word of caution – make sure it is the *employee's* views you are reflecting. It's all too easy for reflective questions to become leading ones.

Leading questions
'Do you *really* think people will consider us more professional because the new accounts clerk has A levels?'

It is obvious that Sarah doesn't, and Paul would have to be pretty confident to argue with the boss. Sarah may be right, but a bad idea can lead to a more productive one; Sarah may also be wrong . . . Leading questions do have their uses, but handle with care!

Multiple questions

'What induction training would you give the new person? Are all the procedures written down, or do they need updating, and will *you* go through all the details or get Martin to show the new person what we do? And how about taking him or her to lunch on the first day, or what if we . . .?'

Have pity on your poor, confused employee – don't use multiple questions.

Types of question

What types of question are these? My answers are given on page 75.

1. How many widgets did we produce last week?
2. What effect did the new process have?
3. Did you use those precise words?
4. Surely you didn't use *those* words?
5. How did you feel when that happened?
6. You sound angry about that – are you?
7. Did he agree with you?
8. Did he confirm his agreement or will he write to let us know formally?
9. Wouldn't it be a good idea to do this?
10. What other effects might there be?

What if you don't get any answer?

We all feel uncomfortable if we ask a question but get no answer – so uncomfortable that we tend to rush in with more words to fill the silence, rephrasing the question, asking another, answering it ourselves. It's worth remembering that, for the employee, the question might take a bit of thought – hence the silence. So press your lips together for a few more moments before breaking the silence yourself.

Prolonged silences, however, *are* very awkward and can put a lot of pressure on people, which may or may not be conducive to successful coaching. It can sometimes be useful to discuss a prolonged silence openly: 'Paul, do you have difficulty answering that question?'

Changing attitudes

At the start of the chapter I said that the purpose of asking questions is to get answers, normally some sort of information. But questions are also an excellent way of changing someone's attitude or behaviour.

For instance, it is useless (and dangerous!) to say 'Don't be so aggressive!' to people who lose their tempers easily. But carefully chosen questions can lead such employees to realise that aggressive behaviour can prevent them from achieving their own objectives.

Read the following scenario and dialogue, and write the questions you would ask at each break point. Write your question in the space provided, before reading the next section of dialogue. These all start with a possible question, together with my comments about it.

Carol is the internal quality assurance auditor, auditing procedures in all departments in the company. She is excellent at identifying defects in the various products and processes, but always seems to annoy the managers and employees of the departments concerned when she brings these defects to their attention. The manager of the distribution department complained to Sarah that Carol seriously upset one of the supervisors when she criticised his delivery rotas. The criticism was justified (rearranging the deliveries could have saved a daily van journey), but the supervisor was so angry at Carol's aggressive behaviour that he nearly walked out. The distribution manager was furious. Sarah asked to see Carol. How would you, as Sarah, start the discussion?

Sarah:

Sarah: Carol, how did the distribution audit go? [Non-judgemental open question, information-seeking.]

Carol: Terrible! They are so slack in distribution – they have no proper systems and the delivery rotas are a complete shambles. Do you know, they have been sending six vans to Birmingham every day for the last nine months when, with a bit of thought, they need only have sent five. That's 300 miles a day, a van *and* a driver's wages that could have been saved.

Sarah:

Sarah: That sounds as if you did a good job of analysing their delivery rotas. What did you do next?
[Fully justified compliment. Another non-judgemental open question.]

Carol: That supervisor, he is *unbelievably* inefficient. When I told him how to rearrange his deliveries, he became completely obstructive and refused to listen. So then I told the manager how badly the deliveries were organised and how rude the supervisor had been. But the manager didn't listen properly either! He's as bad as the supervisor! That department must be costing the company thousands.

Sarah:

Sarah: How do you feel after that audit?
[Again a non-judgemental open question – the first step towards changing Carol's attitude and behaviour.]

Carol: Completely fed up and frustrated. All my hard work wasted.

Sarah:

Sarah: What outcome to the audit would you have liked?
[Open question – the second step.]

Carol: Well, obviously, I wanted them to listen.

Sarah:

Sarah: Is there anything you could have done to get them to listen?
[A closed probe, attempting the third step, but too fast and abrupt.]

Carol: No, they're too stupid.

Sarah:

Sarah: But you would have liked them to listen? Why do you think they didn't?
[Reflective question to re-establish agreement, followed by an open probe.]

Carol: Because they're stupid.

Sarah:

Sarah: Any other reason?
         [Open probe.]

Carol: They don't like their inefficiency being shown
         up.

Sarah:

Sarah: I think you're absolutely right there. I'm sure
         that's the crux of the matter. Do you think they
         actually *want* to be inefficient?
         [Leading question.]

Carol: Well, no, I suppose not.

Sarah:

Sarah: So you and they want the same outcome and are
         really on the same side, aren't you?
         [Reflective/leading question, summarising but
         also presenting new perspective.]

Carol: I hadn't really seen it that way, but I suppose
         you're right.

Sarah:

Sarah: How do you think you can get *them* to see it that way?
[Open question – the third step, and probably quite enough for one coaching discussion. So far, Sarah has not expressed any dissatisfaction at Carol's behaviour or mentioned the distribution manager's complaint. That could be brought in at a later stage in the discussion, in a later coaching discussion, or possibly not even at all.]

Some people may consider this approach too manipulative. Any attempt to change people *is* manipulative, if it is done without the employee's willing participation (and having them learn new attitudes, and also, if less obviously, new skills and knowledge, is indeed changing people). But Carol *was* willing, if only to avoid the frustration she had experienced, and so would most employees be in such situations.

Suggested answers

1. Closed question.
2. Open question.
3. Closed question, probably closed probe.
4. Leading question.
5. Open question.
6. Reflective question.
7. Closed question.
8. Multiple question.
9. Leading question.
10. Open question, probably open probe.

CHAPTER 12
Listening

Summary

- Listening is focused, attentive hearing.
- Most people listen less well than they might.
- We all experience many mental and physical barriers to listening.
- To overcome these barriers:

  Look, and look interested
  Identify the issues
  Suspend judgement
  Test your understanding
  Exclude your emotions
  Notes, noises and non-verbals.

What is listening?

Listening is much more, and much less, than hearing. Hearing is the physical process by which the brain records sounds. You go into a crowded room and hear a babble of noise. Suddenly, one set of sounds – maybe a voice you recognise – catches your attention, and you can not only hear the voice but also distinguish and understand the words. So listening is much more than hearing.

But, because it is selective, it is also much less. In order to tune into that recognised voice, you have tuned out all, or most, of the other voices. The cause of many listening problems lies in our capacity to be selective and tune out part of what we hear.

Importance of listening

Listening is, in many ways, the most important part of the communication process. I may know exactly what I want to say; I may express it clearly; but if you understand it differently . . . The *real* communication is not what I meant, not even what I said, but what you, from your perspective, understood.

How well do we listen?

Think of the years you spent learning to read, write and speak, at school and at home. How much time have you spent learning to listen? Probably, none.

Most people *feel* that they are quite good listeners. But few are. Listening, proper listening, attending and understanding rather than just hearing, is difficult.

One reason is that our selection of what to attend to may lead to bias. A second is that putting ourselves in someone else's position does not come naturally to most of us! And a third reason is that not even the fastest speaker can match our thinking speed, so our attention can easily wander.

How much do you know about listening?

Test yourself with this quiz. Are these statements true or false? Answers are on page 81.

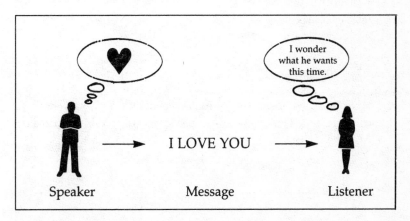

Speaker   Message   Listener

	T/F
1. Most people listen more than they speak.	
2. Good listeners don't say anything while listening.	
3. Good listeners look at the speaker.	
4. People listen well when they feel strongly about the topic.	
5. Listeners are more influenced by what is said than by how it is said.	
6. People listen to criticism.	

Barriers to listening

Many barriers can get in the way of our listening properly. Here are a few, and I am sure you can add others from your own experience:

- Different perspectives
- Strong emotions
- Prejudices
- Mental laziness
- Physical tiredness or discomfort
- Desire to talk
- Distractions and mind wandering
- Reactions to the speaker.

Overcoming these barriers is a matter of deliberately cultivating a good listening technique until it becomes completely natural.

LISTEN

Look, and look interested
Identify the issues
Suspend judgement
Test your understanding
Exclude your emotions
Notes, noises and non-verbals.

Look, and look interested
Speakers need to be looked at or they will rapidly run out of steam. Also, by looking at the speaker, you can 'read' his or her expressions and body language – more about that below.

But looking at the speaker with a bored, glazed expression is not much use. Adopt an attentive position, sitting straight and alert with your head up and your arms uncrossed. It will bring you a bonus – your looking interested will stimulate the speaker to *be* more interesting.

Identify the issues
Even the most skilled speakers will say some things which are not worth listening to. And many speakers are far from skilled – they waffle, they get bogged down on minor issues, they contradict themselves, they lose their track. And, if you're not careful, they lose you too. Stay mentally alert by summarising to yourself what is being said, spotting links with earlier statements, and picking out the main points.

Suspend judgement
However, make sure that, in your anxiety to understand and interpret the essence of what is being said, you don't leap to conclusions. It is amazingly easy to hear what you expect to hear, rather than what is being said, in particular if it's a subject about which you know a lot or have strong feelings.

Certain gestures are common when you are making judgements, for instance chin-stroking, or placing your hand on your cheek with the index finger pointing upwards. Examine your feelings if you catch yourself making these gestures, and be aware that, *even if you don't think you are feeling judgemental,* you may still be giving your employee that impression.

Test your understanding
Check out your assumptions and conclusions along the way, not just at the end of a 20-minute diatribe: 'So what you're saying is . . .', 'Does that mean . . .?'

Don't be afraid to admit early if you haven't understood. We often feel reluctant to interrupt a speaker, but it's better to clarify any uncertainty at once than to miss the whole of the argument.

Exclude your emotions
Your prejudices and your strong feelings about the topic and the speaker will all get in the way of your listening. Very few people can be dispassionate when listening to a subject about which they feel passionately. But it helps to acknowledge any prejudices and feelings in advance, to yourself and sometimes even to the speaker. You can then more easily identify how much they are affecting your reactions, and try to counteract this.

Watch out for body positions which often indicate a critical or negative response (head down, frowning, arms crossed). Your employee will react to your unspoken messages.

Notes, noises and non-verbals
Taking notes has a number of advantages:

- It helps out your memory, and that of your employee.
- It shows that you are taking something seriously.
- It can cool a heated discussion – have you ever tried to shout at dictation speed?

Encouraging noises are one of the listener's greatest tools. 'Mm . . .', 'Yes', 'I see' may not carry much meaning, but they do convey the most important message of all – that you are listening.

These encouraging noises can be considered non-verbal messages since the words are not important. In general, non-verbal messages, those expressed by face, tone of voice, posture and gestures, have much more impact than the words which are used, so they are worth considering carefully.

Reading 'body language' has become almost a game, with gesture alphabets supposedly helping you to identify people's true feelings. It's a dangerous game – single gestures in isolation can very often be misinterpreted, especially across different cultures.

When considering your employee's body language, you have the big advantage of knowing what gestures and expressions are habitual, so your instinctive feelings that Jonathan is uncertain of himself or that Alice is frustrated and angry are probably right. But be cautious, bring your reaction into the open and check out your interpretation – 'Alice, you look fed up. Is anything wrong?'

Also, because people do interpret certain signs fairly predictably, be careful of the signals that you are giving out, particularly any judgemental and critical ones.

Suggested answers

1. True. About two-thirds of face-to-face communication time is spent listening and only a third speaking – but how effective is all that listening?
2. False. Listening is an active process. Good listeners show that they are listening by making encouraging noises and checking their understanding.
3. True. Eye contact is the biggest encouragement of all (and looking away is an excellent method of shutting up a 'waffler'!)
4. False. The strength of their feelings actually gets in the way, as their minds are full of what *they* think (and are planning to say as soon as they can get a word in).
5. False. Research has indicated that people are influenced:

- 7 per cent by the words spoken
- 38 per cent by the way in which they are spoken
- 55 per cent by the way the speaker looks.

If a speaker's words conflict with the non-verbal message given by his or her voice and manner, listeners almost invariably respond to the non-verbal message.

6. False. People do not usually listen well to criticism – hurt, defensive or angry reactions tend to take over, unless the person giving the criticism is particularly skilled.

CHAPTER 13
Observing

Summary

- Observing is focused, attentive seeing.
- Observation may be unreliable because of our mental tendencies to complete the picture and see what we expect.
- Observing is most effective when we:
  - identify in advance what we want to observe
  - observe performance at least twice
  - record the observations.

Optical illusions

The two classic optical illusions shown overleaf illustrate the main problems we have when observing something – context and experience.

1. Which line is the longer?

2. What do you see? Answers are on page 86.

How do we observe?

Just as listening is much more, and much less, than hearing, so observing is much more, and much less, than seeing. When we see a picture, the brain records many visual stimuli to do with composition, colour, technique, etc. But if we choose to observe

Coaching your Employees

1.
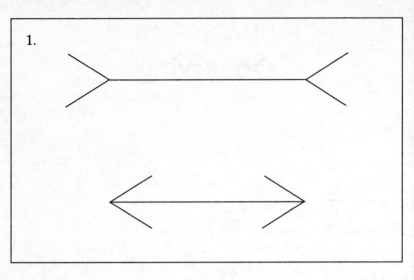

2.
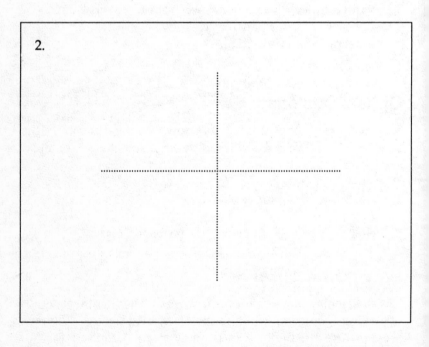

the brushwork attentively, we may no longer take in the composition of the picture.

The same is true of a dynamic scene, such as a television programme. If we are following an exciting police drama, we may miss details such as the registration number, and even the colour, of the getaway van. (On the other hand, if we focus on these, we may miss the action!)

In order to compensate for this selectivity, the brain tries to make sense of what we have observed, by linking up the details we have spotted with extra information based on the context of what we have seen and our experience. This extra information may, or may not, be correct. Thus, I will be convinced that the getaway van:

- Was light blue (because, in the background of the scene, there happened to be a lady wearing a light-blue coat)
- Had the letters E and O in the registration number (because, although I actually saw the shapes F and C, E and O happen to be in the registration number of *my* car, and therefore I associate them with registration numbers, and my brain fills in the extra lines so that I 'see' E and O).

No wonder witness statements can be unreliable and conflicting!

Observing work

When observing an employee's work (so as to identify learning needs or to monitor performance), you need to reduce the effects of context and experience on your observation. To help you do this:

- Identify in advance what details you want to observe.
- Observe performance at least twice, the first time to see the complete action and the second to focus on the details. This will reduce your tendency to complete the picture mentally and see what you expect.

- Record what you have observed – in words, diagrams or even video – for future reference (or to resolve current disagreements).

Charts

Observations can often be charted. This ensures consistency of recording and reduces verbiage! Charts are by no means *always* necessary, but two types are particularly useful when recording repetitive work processes.

Floor plans are used to show how much walking about is involved in completing a particular task. Almost invariably, savings in movement, and hence in time, *can* be made, but be careful in imposing these on employees – the advantages may well be outweighed by the disadvantages of restricting the employees' control over their own work.

Process charts are used to identify and clarify the separate elements in complex processes, especially those which span more than one function or department. They show:

- The flow of work
- What happens to it at each stage in the process
- Links with other processes.

Answers

The two horizontal lines are the same length, but the first *looks* longer because of its context, with the 'whiskers' extending outwards.

The arrangement of dots is usually seen as a cross, as your brain fills in the gaps.

CHAPTER 14
Giving Feedback

Summary

- Feedback is necessary for learning and contributes to motivation.
- All feedback should be:
  - expressed by the employee as well as the coach
  - given as soon as possible after the event
  - given in reasonable quantity
  - considered as information rather than judgement
  - specific and objective
  - 'owned' by the giver.
- Praise should be:
  - given frequently
  - given publicly
  - combined with rewards where possible
  - a reflection of genuine feelings
  - expressed with appropriate body language.
- Criticism should be:
  - given privately
  - avoided when angry
  - mixed with justifiable praise
  - constructive
  - clearly understood
  - expressed with appropriate body language.

Feedback, learning and motivation

Feedback is an essential part of learning. Learning is a continuing cycle of:

- Acquiring new knowledge, skills or attitudes
- Checking their effectiveness through feedback
- Modifying and reacquiring them as appropriate
- Rechecking their effectiveness through more feedback
- Remodifying . . .

Think of babies learning to walk, talk, even to smile. Their progress depends on the continual feedback they get from their parents. And this feedback is essential, not just for the babies' learning but for their psychological well-being. It affirms that they exist and are important.

The Holy Roman Emperor, Frederick II, is said to have wanted to determine which language, Hebrew, Greek or Latin, was innate in human beings, so he devised an experiment. He decreed that a group of infants should be well cared for, but prevented from hearing any human speech from the moment of birth, so that whatever language they began to speak would be their innate language. The result? Not only did the babies fail to speak any language – they died from the lack of interaction.

As with infants, so with adults. Feedback is more than just a tool to aid learning. By affirming our importance, it can motivate us to greater effort and improve our relationship with our manager.

This is true, even if the feedback criticises our performance. If that last statement surprises you, think back to a situation where you received feedback which was helpful and motivating.

Was the feedback congratulatory, critical or mixed?

_____

_____

What were the characteristics of the feedback which made it successful for you?

_____

_____

_____

How do you _now_ feel about the person who gave you the feedback?

_____

_____

_____

Suggestions for giving feedback

Feedback should be:

- Expressed by both employee and coach. The employee often knows quite well how things went. Modesty may inhibit self-praise, but persevere as it is important for the employee to acknowledge success. Self-criticism, too, is valuable and easier for the employee to accept. (Be careful, though, not to let it become a substitute for action.) And always let the employee explain what happened and why, before _you_ give critical feedback – that can save you many a red face!
- Given as soon as possible after the event. The longer you delay, the less impact it has.
- Given in reasonable quantity. Too much is as bad as too little.

Even if the employee's performance is full of faults, focus on only one or two per coaching session.

- Considered as information for the employee's use, not a sentence that you have delivered. That way the relationship between you can be a partnership of equals rather than judge looking down on the prisoner at the bar.
- Specific and objective. Concentrate on the *situation* and what went well or badly, rather than the person. This will help your feedback to be more informational and less judgemental.
- 'Owned' by the giver. Not 'everybody thinks . . .' but 'I saw . . .', 'I heard . . .', 'I think . . .' These statements are more accurate and acknowledge that what you are expressing is your view. That allows the employee to choose more freely how to make use of the feedback.

Praise

A pat on the back is cheap and quick, so why do we give so few? Teachers are advised to praise children five times as often as they criticise, but how often does that happen?

And how many of you have just thought: 'And a good job, too! Praising people all the time makes them complacent and lazy'?

This is the main reason that we don't encourage our employees enough. Our culture devalues praise and encouragement, as though we should be psychologically too strong to need them. But many people these days feel insecure in their jobs; worry then inhibits their performance, which makes them even more anxious. The mundane reality is that encouragement breeds confidence, and confident employees learn best and fastest.

A second reason why we give too little praise is that we take progress, especially gradual progress, for granted, and may not even notice it. It's worth pausing every so often, and asking: 'Could you do this last year, last month, last week?' That is progress, and deserves praise.

As well as the suggestions for giving feedback generally, praise should:

- Be given frequently. Try to catch people doing something right – especially those who always seem to do everything wrong. Praise often. It doesn't debase the currency.
- Be given publicly. The more you publicise your praise, the more effect it has on the employee. Admittedly, embarrassment *can* cause problems, but you know your employee and can decide whether, for example, to put a letter of commendation on the notice-board for all to see, or whether simply to send a copy of it to your own boss.
- Be accompanied by a reward. This doesn't have to be a pay increase! A congratulatory pint, an afternoon off for an employee who has worked long and hard to complete a project, or just a change of tasks can be very effective rewards.
- Reflect your genuine feelings. If you feel grudging or patronising, it will be obvious to your employee whatever your words. Concentrate on expressing genuine appreciation and gratitude (and you *ought* to feel that – if only because an employee's good performance makes your job easier and reflects well upon you as a manager!).
- Use open body language (smiling expression, head up, leaning slightly forward, arms not crossed or folded) to reinforce your message.

Criticism

When giving criticism, *think positive*. Criticism is not, as it is often called, negative feedback: it should, ultimately if not immediately, be seen as a positive, helpful experience. As well as the general suggestions for feedback, criticism should:

- Be given privately. Public criticism is usually humiliating and therefore counter-productive. You may have to delay the criticism in order to give it in private – only you can decide whether immediacy or privacy are more important in a particular situation.
- Be avoided while you are feeling angry. Count to ten, walk round the block, get a cup of coffee, but *calm down before you criticise*.

- Be mixed with justifiable praise. Very few performances are unrelievedly bad, and genuine praise for what did go well makes your criticism more balanced and more easily accepted.
- Be constructive and encouraging. Focus on how to put things right and avoid similar errors in the future. Try and build on the employee's poor ideas and performance to develop better ones.
- Be clearly understood. Talk straight and don't dodge the issue.
- Avoid negative or judgemental body language (frowning, head down, arms crossed). Try to adopt a more open posture.

Some situations

What would you say, as Paul, in the following situations? My suggestions are given opposite.

1. Ann has been struggling for a long time to get right the median calculations for the monthly report. Every time there has been some mistake or other. At last she has completed it without mistakes.

2. Paul has asked John (this is pre-Friday the 13th!) to do a rather boring job which has to be ready first thing next morning. It hasn't been done. John apologises – he forgot. He often seems to 'forget' or 'not have time for' the boring jobs.

3. Martin has just completed a rush job as a favour for Paul. It meant that he had to drop everything else he was doing, which will cause him much more work later on. There are several mistakes in the job Martin has done.

Suggested answers

Paul should:

1. Show his delight with enthusiastic praise, maybe informing Sarah, and making sure Ann knows that he has done this.
2. Tell John straight out that he has let him down. Paul should make sure John realises to what trouble he has put Paul, and possibly other people. As soon as Paul has the time, he should:

   - Talk with John about what his job entails
   - Find out if John has any problems with it
   - Possibly reallocate tasks, but only if this makes sense within the context of the whole department
   - Make sure John realises that *all* jobs contain boring but necessary elements.

3. Thank Martin and tell him how grateful he feels to him for putting himself out to help. Unless Paul will never again want Martin's help, he should *not* point out the errors now, but correct them himself. Paul may want to discuss any habitual errors with Martin later.

CHAPTER 15
Explaining

Summary

Effective explanations should:

- Consider the employee's perspective
- Establish the importance of the topic to the listener
- Check understanding
- Repeat the message
- Record important details in writing.

Bob's problem

Bob has just been recruited to replace John. Ann is explaining to Bob how to use the word-processing software.

Ann:	This is the word-processing menu, Bob. To create a document, press C for create, give it a document name, and press Return. Type up your document and, when you have finished, press Exit, S for save and Return. To delete or print, it's D or P. OK?
Bob:	Er, yes.
Ann:	Then I'll leave you to it.
Bob (thinks):	I do hate computers. I would much rather write things out in longhand. But everyone uses word processors now, and I don't want to seem stupid.

> Bob (thinks later, after creating and typing up his document): Well, that wasn't so bad, I suppose. Now what do I do? Oh, yes, Ann said press Exit and S for save, D for delete or P for print. This was a practice run so I'll press D. Why isn't anything happening? Perhaps I got it wrong and should press a different key. What about this one labelled DEL? That must stand for delete, surely. Oh, help, now I've got a funny message on the screen: 'Do you really want to delete this program? If so, press DEL again.' I suppose I do – at least I want to delete my document. Should I ask Ann but I don't want her to consider me an idiot. She seems to think it's all so easy. Oh well, I'll press DEL again . . . Oh, no, the screen has gone completely blank. What have I deleted?

You may consider that unbelievably badly constructed word-processing software (I would agree with you!), but don't consider Ann's explanation or Bob's nervousness and naïvety to be unbelievable. This is a real situation.

What do you think was wrong with Ann's explanation? My answers are on pages 98–9.

- •

- •

- •

- •

- •

- •

Employee perspective

Ann's explanation had a number of faults, but the biggest was that she didn't put herself in Bob's place. Her explanation, faults and all, could have been adequate for someone who was familiar with computers, and had no qualms about asking questions if anything unexpected occurred.

To show you how easily explanations can go wrong, try this exercise on a colleague. Tell your colleague that the vertical line in the figure below represents the letter 'i'. Now tell your colleague to put a dot on the 'i'.

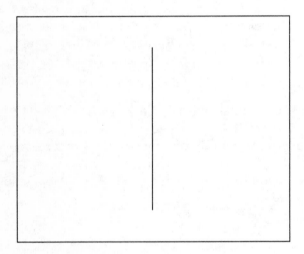

Anybody who put a dot above the straight line (as in 'i'), did not follow the instructions, which were to put a dot *on* the straight line which represents the letter i.

This is obviously a trick question, and people are on their guard. Nevertheless, most people still get the exercise wrong, because the instructions don't take account of an adult's acquired knowledge of writing 'i's and of the common phrase 'dotting the i' – the words are fine for 3–5-year-old children!

Suggestions for effective explanations

- Consider and structure them from the employee's viewpoint.
- Establish the importance of the topic to the employee.
- Break the explanation up into digestible chunks.
- Use simple, accurate terms.
- Check understanding at frequent intervals, and encourage the employee to ask questions, now or later.
- Follow the old trainer's adage – 'First you tell them what you're going to tell them, then you tell them, then you tell them what you told them.'
- Record important details in writing for future reference. By the way, be aware that a sizeable proportion of the workforce is not literate. If any of your employees fall into this category, use diagrams rather than words. This is particularly important for safety notices.

Bob's problem avoided

Let's give Ann another chance!

Ann:	This is the word-processing menu, Bob. Are you familiar with word processors?
Bob:	No, not really.
Ann:	Then I'll just take you through the basic facilities. Do ask if you have any questions. First I'll show you how to create a document. This menu tells you what to do – you have to press C for create. Then a message on the screen asks you to enter your document name – just type it in. Then press Return. You must press Return every time you want the computer to perform any action, like creating, saving, printing or deleting a document. So, are you clear on how to create a document?
Bob:	Yes, I press C, then type in the document name, and press Return.

Ann:	Right. Then you type up your document. For the moment just use the keyboard as a typewriter and I'll go over the special word-processing functions with you later. When you've finished, you tell that to the computer by pressing Exit. OK?
Bob:	Yes, fine.
Ann:	You may want to save your document on disc so that you can retrieve it later. To do that, press S for save (do you see it on the menu?) and Return. Looking at the menu, what keys do you think you should press to print a document?
Bob:	P.
Ann:	And?
Bob:	Oh yes, Return.
Ann:	That's right. And to delete a document?
Bob:	D and Return.
Ann:	Good. As you see, the menu tells you what to do, but here's a list of the main functions and the keys you should press. By the way, be particularly careful not to press the DEL key if you want to delete your document – you may find yourself deleting the computer software instead! OK?
Bob:	Yes, no problems.
Ann:	Good. But don't worry if something does go wrong – it usually does to start with. Just give me a shout if anything funny happens.

Suggested answers

Ann did not:

- Identify how Bob felt about the task (nervous, reluctant).
- Identify what Bob already knew about word processing (nil).
- Identify the purpose of the explanation.

- Check Bob's understanding of the explanation.
- Clearly express what had to be done to delete and print documents (pressing D or P, *and then pressing Return*).
- Summarise the main points of the explanation.
- Give Bob written details for reference.
- Anticipate and warn Bob about any likely difficulties.
- Encourage Bob to consult her if he met with any problems.

CHAPTER 16
Demonstrating

Summary

- Demonstration is the best way of learning skills.
- Demonstration consists of:
  - preparation
  - modelling the desired behaviour
  - the employee trying the behaviour
  - feedback.

Nellie

Demonstration is the best way of learning skills. But demonstrating, itself, is more of a skill than you might first think.

Learners through the years have 'sat next to Nellie', watching and copying another employee with varying degrees of success. Problems have arisen because:

- The learner didn't properly observe and duplicate Nellie's performance.
- The learner didn't have the chance to observe infrequently performed tasks.
- The learner didn't understand the context of the task, so could not respond to unexpected situations.
- Nellie wasn't always good at her job.
- Nellie didn't always choose the most effective way of carrying out the task.

Successful demonstrating is more than just Nellie-watching. The demonstration process has four main stages:

1. Preparation
2. Modelling the desired behaviour
3. Having the employee try the behaviour
4. Giving feedback.

Steps 3 and 4 or 2, 3 and 4 can be repeated as often as necessary.

Preparation

Both the coach and the employee need to be prepared. The coach has to:

- Structure the demonstration in the best way for the employee to learn. Break the task down into ideally no more than eight steps – more than that will be difficult for the employee to absorb in a single session.

  This applies equally to interpersonal skills. A training method called 'behaviour modelling' uses this approach to help people deal with difficult situations.

One of Bob's tasks is to chase customers who haven't paid their accounts. Paul has broken this task down into seven steps for Bob.

1. After 28 days, send standard reminder letter.
2. If the account is still unpaid, phone the customer seven days later.
3. Check that the account and letter have been received.
4. Explain the company policy – any customers who have had an account outstanding for more than 42 days have to pay in advance for any future orders.
5. Explain that you have phoned because they are valued

> customers, and you want to ensure that they are not in-
> convenienced in this way.
>
> 6. Get commitment to pay within seven days, or refer to
> your supervisor.
> 7. Confirm the phone call in writing.

- Set up the physical environment for the demonstration. It is *not* conducive to learning to interrupt a demonstration because of telephone calls, 'urgent' messages, lack of equipment or mislaid documents!
- Explain the demonstration process to the employee.
- Explain the purpose and context of the task to the employee.

Modelling the desired behaviour

As coach, you may do this yourself, you may get a suitable Nellie or an expert in another department to do it, or you may use video.

Videos of the successful approach in action are particularly common in training courses using behaviour modelling, but you can also use them on a one-to-one basis. If many employees need to learn the same skill, you may even want to create your own video. It is often better, in that case, to film real work in progress (watch for a fairly long period before you start filming, in order to dispel embarrassment and awkwardness) than to stage an event or role play specially for the camera, as these can seem unreal. If you want help in creating a video, consult your training department.

Incidentally, remember that your own continuing behaviour is the most powerful model of all for employees developing their communication and supervisory skills. Just as we tend to bring up our children as our parents brought us up, so we manage like our managers.

Trying the behaviour

You can place as many safeguards on this as you wish. Letting the employee try does *not* mean letting him or her loose, unsupervised, on your best customer! Trials can be:

- Off the job, as a role play or using training facilities. Role plays can range from videoed set pieces to a quick run-through of a potentially difficult meeting. Training facilities can be as sophisticated as computer-controlled simulators, or as everyday as an ordinary telephone.
- Supervised, so that any disastrous errors are prevented before they happen.
- For real, in safe, low-risk situations.
- For real, in more critical situations.

As the employees' skills develop, so the potential riskiness of the trial can be increased.

Feedback

This is inherent in the demonstration process and should be given as soon as possible after the trial. See Chapter 14 for suggestions on how to give feedback.

CHAPTER 17
Setting Goals and Standards

Summary

- Goals and standards of performance define what, and how well, an employee is expected to perform.
- Goals and standards should:
  - be agreed by the manager and employee
  - describe end-results
  - be specific and, ideally, measurable
  - reflect the desired level of performance
  - be expressed in writing.

Comparing goals and standards

Setting goals and standards of performance is the single, most effective means of improving that performance. Goals and standards essentially serve the same purpose – defining what, and how well an employee is expected to perform. The main difference between them is that goals are used to define the performance of a one-off task in the future, whereas standards are used for regular, continuing tasks. Goals, therefore, usually have an end-date for the task, while standards do not. This difference, however, is less important than their shared characteristics. Goals and standards should:

- Be agreed jointly by manager and employee
- Describe end-results
- Be specific and, ideally, measurable

- Reflect the desired level of performance
- Be expressed in writing.

Nationally recognised standards now exist for many jobs.

Manager/Employee agreement

Goals and standards which you impose on an employee work less well than those which you agree jointly. In particular, employees are most likely to be committed to goals and standards *they* have suggested. Even with external standards, you and your employee can agree whether to accept the standards as they are written, or whether to modify them to suit your situation.

The process of reaching joint agreement is, in fact, very valuable in itself. It is amazing how often manager and employee have very different perceptions of the employee's job, and simply clarifying expectations can resolve many performance problems.

End-results

Goals and standards should describe the desired end-result and the employee's role in achieving this, not the specific activities which the employee must perform. For example, 'keep my manager regularly informed of the progress of my work', rather than 'complete a monthly report', even though that is what the employee might actually *do*.

Do the following phrases describe end-results or activities? Answers at the end of the chapter.

1. Hold annual performance appraisal discussions.
2. Keep employees fully informed.
3. Improve staff morale.
4. Talk to each employee daily.
5. Set up a department notice-board.
6. Hold weekly department meetings.

This may seem like quibbling over words, but the principle is important. Goals and standards which describe activities are:

- Restrictive (since they imply that no other actions are acceptable).
- Exceedingly long-winded (since they have to cover *all* required activities).
- Ultimately, *inhibiting* of initiative, learning and development.

Measurement

One of the reasons we sometimes find it easier to express goals and standards in terms of activities, rather than results, is that these are, by their nature, more specific. But end-result statements also need to be made specific, so that you and the employee can assess whether or not they have been achieved.

It is certainly possible to make verbal descriptions specific, but they tend to be very lengthy. The best way to be specific is to use numbers. As is often said: 'What gets measured, gets done.'

Many people protest that 'intangible' end-results such as employee morale or communication are not measurable, but these are precisely the ones that most need measurement. And it's surprising how many measurements *can* be found.

List some measurements of employee morale. Suggested answers are given on page 108.

-
-
-
-
-
-
-

However, do use your common sense about any measurements which depend on complicated monitoring systems. You are trying to improve performance, not create additional administration.

Performance level

This is a juggling act. Goals and standards need to be:

- Achievable. There's nothing more demotivating than setting the employee up for failure by requiring a completely unattainable level of performance.
- Challenging. However, if the goals and standards are *too* easily achieved, employees will again feel demotivated and won't develop to their full potential. Your expectations are the key. If you expect average or below average performance, that's what you are likely to get; high (but reasonable) expectations are what create superior performance.

Written documents

Goals and standards need to be written down because that:

- Helps to clarify your intent
- Brings out any underlying differences between you and your employee
- Serves as a record for future reference.

Writing down your goals and standards does *not* have to mean using elaborate forms – the simpler your record the better. The following example is straightforward to complete and use.

Goal/standard	Measurement	Target date	When achieved	Comments

Suggested answers

1. Activity.
2. End-result.
3. End-result.
4. Activity.
5. Activity.
6. Activity.

Some ways of measuring employee morale (page 106) are:

- Employee attitude surveys
- Length of service of employees
- Number of employee suggestions for improving work performance
- Number of performance appraisals held (and their outcomes)
- Number of employees requesting training
- Employee turnover (and reasons for leaving)
- Absenteeism and lateness
- Number of employee grievances (and their outcomes).

CHAPTER 18
Gaining Commitment

Summary

Employee commitment comes from:

- Your ongoing relationship with your employees
- Your management style and that of your organisation
- Your coaching skills
- Your own commitment to coaching and to your employees.

More than good intentions

Setting goals and standards, however useful an exercise it may be in itself, should only be the first step. What counts most is achieving them.

But how often have you, with the best will in the world, set yourself goals and yet, somehow, not done anything about them? Commitment is more than good intentions. And some employees, for whatever reason, may not even have good intentions. We have all known the employee whose mouth says 'Yes, of course', but whose eyes and general bearing give out a very qualified 'maybe, if you're lucky'!

Management style

So how do you gain commitment? Unfortunately, you can't just pull it out of a hat at the end of a coaching session like a magic rabbit – it is the product of your ongoing relationship with your employees. The more open and democratic your relationships and your (and your organisation's) management style, the more naturally coaching fits into them, and the more committed your employees are likely to be.

	More true than false		More false than true	
	Dept	Orgn	Dept	Orgn
Management:				
• Is supportive of employees' desire to progress and develop.				
• Is easy to talk to, even when under pressure.				
• Gives employees all the information they want.				
• Has consistently high expectations of employees.				
• Accepts genuine mistakes without recrimination.				
• Gives credit for work well done.				
• Has long- and short-term goals and objectives.				
• Trusts employees to get on with a job without constant supervision.				
• Delegates authority and responsibility as well as tasks.				
• Considers team and individual performance to be of primary importance.				

Opposite is a list of statements describing management style. Identify how representative you think each one is of your own department, section or unit, and of your organisation as a whole by ticking the relevant column. (If you're brave enough, get your employees to do the same thing and compare your answers!)

The more ticks you have in the first two columns, the more conducive the management style is to successful coaching.

Ticks in the third column are up to you – you are the best person to influence and modify the management style in your department or section.

As for the fourth column, you might do worse than to leave a copy of this book in a prominent position on your managing director's desk!

Skills

With this basis, you can generate commitment by using the coaching skills we have already discussed:

- Making time to coach, and being seen by employees to treat it as a high priority
- Considering each individual and his or her learning needs
- Finding, or making, coaching opportunities which meet the learning needs
- Asking questions, to bring out information and contribute to attitude change
- Listening to the answers, actively
- Observing performance, closely and accurately
- Giving feedback, honestly and constructively
- Explaining information, clearly and with understanding of the employee's perspective
- Demonstrating skills, with careful thought and planning
- Setting realistic, yet challenging, goals and standards.

Your commitment

And, finally, to generate commitment you must demonstrate your own commitment. Your commitment to coaching – remember the benefits.

For you:

- A more successful and productive department
- Greater confidence when delegating tasks to your employees
- Development of your own management skills
- A growing reputation as a 'developer of people'
- Less time-consuming firefighting, allowing you to spend more time on your own development.

Leading, possibly, to:

- Promotions and salary increases!

For your employees:

- The recognition of their importance to you, the department and the company
- The development of their skills
- Growing satisfaction as they improve their performance
- Greater interest in their tasks
- Greater independence and responsibility for their work
- A growing ability to take on more varied, interesting and challenging tasks.

Leading, possibly, to:

- Promotions and salary increases!

For your company:

- Better motivated employees and managers

- Better developed employees and managers.

Leading, definitely, to:

- Better quality products and processes
- Greater profits.

Consider also your foundation-stone, your commitment to your employees. Commitment is built on trust and respect – your employees' trust and respect for you, and yours for them. Without that, you may go through the motions of coaching, but neither of you will have enough confidence in the other, or in the coaching process between you, to allow full commitment.

The checklists in the final section of this book are there to help you hone your skills. The action plan will help you put it all into practice. Do so, for your own sake, and for that of your employees and your company – and build your staircase to success!

CHAPTER 19
Checklists

Preparing to coach

	OK	Could do better	*Should do better*
How well do I:			
• Find time to coach?			
• Identify the employee's learning needs?			
• Identify specific learning objectives for the required knowledge, skills or attitudes?			
• Decide what sort of coaching approach will best meet the learning needs?			
• Decide who should coach the employee?			
• Plan suitable coaching opportunities?			
• Spot suitable coaching opportunities as they occur?			
• Get employees to identify suitable coaching opportunities for themselves?			
• Ensure employees have the necessary resources and authority to carry out the task?			

Briefing discussion

	OK	Could do better	*Should do better*
How well do I: • Pick my moment to suit the employee? • Set up the environment to encourage free discussion? • Explain briefly and clearly what needs doing, without dictating how? • Agree goals for both the task and the learning? • Ask open questions to establish how well the employee understands the situation? • Ask questions to bring out the employee's suggestions about how to tackle the task? • Get the employee to do about half the talking? • Listen to the employee? • Use encouraging body language? • Demonstrate the task, where this is necessary?			

Monitoring the task

	OK	Could do better	*Should do better*
How well do I: • Give the employee sufficient support? • Give the employee sufficient freedom? • Allow mistakes (in moderation)? • Observe performance, methodically and at least twice? • Record performance?			

Review discussion

	OK	Could do better	*Should* do better
How well do I: • Pick my moment to suit the employee? • Set up the environment to encourage free discussion? • Ask questions to establish how well the employee thinks the task and learning objectives were achieved? • Get the employee to set or agree goals for further improvement and for practising what has been learnt? • Get the employee to identify how well I supported him/her? • Get the employee to do about three-quarters of the talking? • Give constructive praise? • Give constructive criticism? • Listen to the employee? • Use encouraging body language?			

Following up

	OK	Could do better	*Should do better*
How well do I: • Set appointments for following up? • Keep those appointments? • Identify further learning needs through the follow-up discussions?			

CHAPTER 20
Your Action Plan

Do you want to improve your coaching skills? Pick two to three activities which you would like to work on, and complete this action plan. Make a contract with yourself to carry out each activity a certain number of times within the next day/week/ month (choose your own time-scale, but make it fairly short). Check off each time you carry out the activity, and then review your performance with your own coach, manager or employees.

Coaching your Employees

Coaching activity which I want to improve	I will do this		Check off each time carried out	Review by (date)/ with (coach etc)
	no of times	by (date)		

Further Reading from Kogan Page

Also by Nancy Stimson: *How to Write and Prepare Training Materials*
Creative Thinking in Business, Carol Kinsey Goman
Delegating for Results, Robert B Maddux
Don't Do. Delegate!, J M Jenks and J M Kelly
Effective Employee Participation, Lynn Tylczak
The First Time Manager, M J Morris
How To Be an Even Better Manager, 3rd edition, Michael Armstrong
How to Develop a Positive Attitude, Elwood N Chapman
How to Motivate People, Twyla Dell
Improving Relations at Work, Elwood N Chapman
Project Management: From Idea to Implementation, Marion E Haynes
Team Building, Robert B Maddux